Kindle Cash System

Getting Started

This book is called the Kindle Cash System.

It occurs to me the title of this book may appear somewhat confusing when you look at the contents. Even though most of the information included here doesn't deal directly with Kindle, this book was put together specifically with Kindle publishers in mind.

Just about every piece of advice I've read concerning self-publishing says the same thing. Keep your book exclusive to Amazon. That's where the majority of the buyers are, so why publish anyplace else?

Makes sense, doesn't it?

Maybe. Maybe not.

. . . .

Think about it this way. If 65 percent of eBook buyers are on Amazon, that still leaves 35 percent - or about one third of all eBook buyers unable to purchase your book.

It also doesn't account for the readers who prefer the feel of paper in their hands. I prefer Kindle, but I know a lot of people who only read paperbacks. And, don't forget, there's a growing market out there for audio books. A lot of people don't like to read, or don't have time for it, but they do like to listen.

Sure you can comfort yourself knowing they can still read your Kindle book on their tablet, iPhone, or laptop— if they download the appropriate app. Some people will do that, probably not the guy who owns a Nook or iPad. He paid good money for that device, and he expects a book made for it. Can't blame him for that, can you?

And then, there are guys like my dad. He's 86 years old. He won't touch a computer, Kindle, smartphone or any of these new-fangled devices. His books have always been made from paper, and they always will be.

And my neighbor, he's always on the road. He's a traveling salesman and he's always in his car, or hopping on a plane for who knows where. He doesn't have time to read, but he does have time to listen.

It's a crazy mixed up world out there. People get their information in a lot of different ways. If you want to reach them, you've got to serve your book up the way they want it.

What I'm trying to say is, don't put all of your eggs in one basket.

Kindle may be the big kid on the block today, but tomorrow is wide open. Amazon may close its doors. The Surgeon General may force Amazon to stamp a warning on every Kindle device stating "they cause eye strain, physical damage to your eyes, or blindness." You never know what's around the next corner.

This book is going to be short and to the point. It's going to show you how to make your book available on a number of the most popular self-publishing platforms.

You don't have to jump in and try all of them at once.

Try one. See how it works for you. Make all of your books available through Smashwords, or in paperback. Sit back and examine the results. When you're ready, try releasing a few of your books in another format. If you're happy with the results, roll all of your books out in that format.

Keep an eye out for new publishing trends. Test a few of them out. Keep the ones that work for you, eliminate the ones that don't.

Over time you will sell more books, because your books are available to more people in the formats they enjoy consuming them in.

....

Authors Note: A good part of this book was first published in my book, *Indie Author's Toolbox*. I decided to reprise it here as the first volume of the *Kindle Cash System* series, because it contains information self-publishers need to read – today.

Its' a big world out there, and no one can say for sure what book marketing methods are going to work best.

Some authors swear by Facebook and Twitter. Other authors live by their mailing list, their blog, or their website. Most authors just turn their book loose, and hope for the best.

It doesn't matter which type of author you are. Every author can benefit from the information contained in this book. The reason is simple. No matter how many people you tell about your book, and no matter how many people want your book, sales don't happen until readers are able to find and purchase your book.

It stands to reason the more places your book is available, the more people are going to discover it, buy it – and, hopefully read it, and tell other people about it.

That's why I decided to repackage this information, and make it available on a wider scale. This new edition has a section on Kobo, Lulu, and a newly revised section on how to use

Babelcube. I've also included more tips and tricks for using each platform.

Kindle Unlimited, Amazon's new subscription reading service is another new factor in the market. Some authors love it, others think it's unfair, and is another way for Amazon to make money off of their hard work. My thought is it's there. At the current time, there's money to be made using it, so you need to understand what it is, how it works, and how it can help you sell more books. For that reason I have included a section on *Kindle Unlimited*.

What this book doesn't have is information about how to publish to the iStore. There are two reasons for this. 1) I don't have a Mac, so I haven't had an opportunity to play around with publishing to the iStore, and 2) For the time being I decided using a book aggregator such as Smashwords or Draft2Digital wasn't such a bad choice for getting my book listed in the iStore.

....

Finally, I want to share the biggest discovery I've made from selling my books on other platforms.

The readers I'm gaining are split pretty much evenly between foreign countries and America. Canadians are a big portion of my new found readers, especially from Google Play and the iStore. There's a smattering of sales trickling in from all over Europe, and quite a few from Australia. These are the readers I'm missing out on by remaining exclusive to Amazon.

I've discovered a number of books that are dead in the water on Amazon sell quite well on these other sites. I don't really have an explanation for it, but it's a pleasant byproduct of having my books available there.

The big question over the next six months is if selling on these other platforms will make up for, or exceed the loss in revenue I forfeit from giving up Amazon exclusivity.

What I mean by this is, will those extra sales cover the lost income I normally receive from KDP borrows and running Kindle Countdown Deals?

. . . .

Another development since I first published this book is *Kindle Unlimited*. In the few short months since its inception, *Kindle Unlimited* has changed the face of self-publishing. I used to receive fifteen or twenty borrows a month under KOLL, which was just a minor portion of my book sales. Now with *Kindle Unlimited* forty to forty-five percent of my sales come from borrows. And, that's after just four months. If it keeps growing at that pace borrows could far outnumber sales in the next six months or less.

So, when you look at selling on other platforms—you really need to understand how it's going to affect your sales. If half of your sales come from *Kindle Unlimited* borrows, that's going to severely affect your author ranking and income if you pull your books out of exclusivity with Amazon.

I don't have an answer for that now, just understand—if you're an indie author, and your books aren't in Kindle Unlimited, you better have a plan to make up those lost sales.

Table of Contents

Kindle Unlimited

I published Kindle Cash System less than six months ago. In the short period of time since then Amazon has once again transformed the face of digital publishing by introducing *Kindle Unlimited*. If you're not familiar with it, *Kindle Unlimited* is a subscription based service that allows readers to choose an unlimited number of books to read. The only limitations are the books must be enrolled in KDP to qualify, and subscribers are limited to ten borrows at any given time.

Kindle Unlimited also gives subscribers access to more than 2300 select audio books, and you can bet that number will continue to grow as the platform matures. The best thing about these audio books is listeners are not required to sign up at audible.com to listen to them. You just select the audio book you want to listen to, and the audio book and the eBook are downloaded to your Kindle device. They operate with Amazon's *Whispersync* technology, so the book or the audio open at the same point. This allows you to easily switch between reading and listening.

The selection of books available through *Kindle Unlimited* right now is skewed more towards indie authors whose books

1

are enrolled in KDP, but you can rest assured this will change as more Kindle users subscribe to the service. Amazon will be forced to add more mainstream books to compete with Oyster and Scribd.

At the current time indie authors have a huge advantage by being part of the *Kindle Unlimited* Program. When your book is available through *Kindle Unlimited*, there's no financial barrier for readers to sample your work. That takes price out of the equation when you're trying to hook new readers. It's also an awesome workaround for the limited promotion times available to authors using *KDP Free* Days or *Kindle Countdown Deals*.

From what I've seen, erotica authors get this best. Nearly every erotica book I've examined includes a call to action in the front or back matter encouraging readers to grab the author's other books for free if they are *Kindle Unlimited* subscribers. The author bios start and end with a mention about *Kindle Unlimited*. The book descriptions start or end by mentioning you can pick up a copy of this book for free if you're a *Kindle Unlimited* subscriber.

How about you? Are you doing everything you can to let readers know they can read all of your books for free? If you're not, you're leaving book sales and additional readers on the table.

Kindle Unlimited for Authors

As an author, you're going to love or hate *Kindle Unlimited*. You might waver back and forth, feeling one reaction and then the other.

The good thing about *Kindle Unlimited* is it moves more books. The bad thing about *Kindle Unlimited* is it moves more books at a lower royalty rate. Six months ago the royalty rate for KOLL borrows averaged $2.11 per book. In October of 2014 the royalty paid for KOLL borrows was $1.51. That's a decrease of 60¢, even with Amazon continuously pumping more money into the program.

The question for authors obviously is, "How low can it go?"

Amazon designed a lucrative bonus program to reward top sellers, but if you're not one of the authors who receives a bonus for having the most borrows, where are you going to draw the line? For the first month or two of *Kindle Unlimited* I was pumped—my book sales climbed by nearly 300 books per month. Four months into the program sales have returned to their normal level, except now—forty to forty-five percent of my sales come from borrows—borrows that I make less royalties on. Not good! Not good at all!

So what's an author supposed to do?

One answer is to toss your hands in the air and pull all of your books out of the program, but that's probably not the best solution. Smart authors understand that sometimes it's best to go with the flow. Subscriber based reading services like *Oyster*, *Scribd*, and *Kindle Unlimited* are here to stay. Rather than fight them, author's need to make the necessary changes to ensure they receive the most borrows and royalties from them.

If you have any doubts whether Amazon is committed to *Kindle Unlimited* or not, you can take a cue from their most recent actions. During the last few months Amazon has rolled the program out in the UK and Germany. I received a notice today (11/04/2014) that *Kindle Unlimited* is now live in Spain and Italy. That means Amazon will likely roll the program out across all of its sites by early next year if not sooner.

My sales are up significantly in the UK and Germany already, mostly due to KOLL borrows. I would expect that trend to continue in Spain and Italy.

Smart authors are going to have one of those V8 moments where they think—What if my books were available in

German, Spanish, or Italian language editions? Would my sales shoot up even more? It's possible. Watch your English edition sales in those countries, and if sales suddenly take off they may be telling you it's time to think about a translated edition. Unfortunately, Babelcube isn't the answer if you're trying to catch the wave with *Kindle Unlimited* borrows. They make their translations available on platforms other than Amazon. The only answer is to commission a translated edition on your own.

. . . .

I've read a lot of half-baked schemes about how to make money with *Kindle Unlimited*. Perhaps one of the dumbest ideas I read suggested authors flood Amazon with short twenty to thirty page books, because readers only have to open ten percent of the book for the author to be paid. The thought was with such short books readers only had to flip through one or two pages for you to get paid full royalties for writing a crappy book.

Don't do that!

If you want to make money with *Kindle Unlimited*, the answer is smart marketing.

Remember what I said earlier that erotica writers really get it. What we all need to do is start marketing like porn stars. And, no—I don't mean you have to write smut, or do nasty things. What you need to do is spread the word. Let everyone who finds your books know they can read some or all of them for free if they are members of *Kindle Unlimited*.

If you check the opening of my Kindle books you'll see I have a *Kindle Unlimited* section that explains the program. It tells readers you can get this and many of my other books for free, and it provides a list of my available books with clickable links.

Did you know—if you're a Kindle Unlimited subscriber you can read this book and many of my other books for free.

To read this book for free, select **read for free** in the order box and it will be delivered to your Kindle reading device for absolutely no charge.

Here are some of my other eBooks available through Kindle Unlimited.

It's one of the first things readers see when they click on my *Look inside* sample. It takes all of the risk out of buying my book if they are members of *Kindle Unlimited* because they know they can read the book for free. It also alerts readers that I have plenty of other books they can read for free.

I've included the same information at the top or bottom of many of my book descriptions…

Remember—if you're a Kindle Unlimited subscriber you can read this book and many of my other books for free. To read this book for free, select Read for Free in the order box and it will be delivered to your Kindle reading device for absolutely no charge.

Once again, it alerts potential readers that they can explore my book with absolutely no costs or risks involved. Hopefully, it makes it easier for readers to say, "Okay, I'll take a chance on this guy."

Not to belabor the point, but I say the same thing again on my Amazon Author page.

Most of my books are available for free if you're a Kindle Unlimited subscriber so feel free to load up your Kindle and read them all.

My books offer short easy to read solutions to your ecommerce problems.

Most of them can be read in under an hour. The information can be used to help you sell more products on eBay and Amazon, services on Fiverr, or eBooks on Amazon and Kindle.

Selling on line isn't a mystery. It doesn't even have to be difficult.

It's really all about getting started. Many people I've talked with have this crazy fear about putting things up for sale on eBay and Amazon. They think they have to do this and do that; they worry they don't know enough about what they're doing to do it right; they wonder what they should sell; and they worry about whether they can even do it or not.

That's where my books come in.

They take you hand-in-hand and walk you through getting started selling on eBay, Amazon, and Fiverr. They show you how to market your Kindle book.

My goal is to help you over the speed bumps, so you can be more successful from the get-go.

What are you waiting for?

Tell people at every entry point into your books that they can read them for free if they are *Kindle Unlimited* subscribers. It will bring you more borrows and sales.

Create Space

Everyone should have some of their books available as a paperback. Even if you have no plans to sell them as paperbacks, or nobody buys them in paperback.

Here's why.

Just having a physical copy of your book can make you and the rest of the world feel more like you're a real writer. There's something about having a paperback copy of your book available that screams out – "Yeah! I'm a writer."

When someone asks you what you write, being able to hand them a hard copy of your book makes it more impressive. Especially if the alternative is telling them, "You can find me on Kindle." That seems a little wimpy compared with being able to put an actual book in their hands.

Finally, you need to offer physical copies of your book to score some Goodreads reviews. They don't let you giveaway eBooks, just paperbacks. So get with the program. Get your paperback made today.

. . . .

Create Space is an Amazon company that gives authors a low cost option for producing paperback versions of their books.

Getting started with Create Space is easy.

Create Space lets authors choose from fifteen different trim sizes. Most authors are going to choose either 6 x 9 or 5.5 x 8. If you're writing nonfiction, stick with 6 x 9. It's the standard size for a trade paperback. If you're writing fiction, 5 x 8 or 5.5 x 8 is going to better resemble what most readers are used to. If you're novel is short, the smaller size will make your book appear bigger. If you're putting together a larger picture oriented book, 8.5 x 11 might be a better choice.

After you've chosen a trim size for your book you need to format it. The easiest way to format your Create Space book is to use MS Word.

The first step is to choose a font. Professionals recommend Garamond or Book Antiqua for paperback books. If you're on the line about which font to choose, format a chapter of your book using each font and decide which one you like best. Another option is to poll several of your friends to determine which typestyle they think looks more professional.

After this you need to set up your page margins. Go to Page Layout – Size – More paper sizes, and manually select the page size you want. I normally set my margins to 1.00 all around. Keep in mind if you have a larger book you may want to adjust this to fit more text on each page. Create Space charges you based on how many pages are in your book so the fewer pages in your book, the less it's going to cost to print.

To number your pages, go to Insert – Page Number, and select the style of page numbers you want to use. I like to use Bottom of Page – Accent Bar 1 because I can include the book title at the bottom of every page.

Choose your line spacing and paragraph indents. Most nonfiction books use block spacing with a line between paragraphs. Works of fiction generally use paragraph indents with no space between paragraphs. I use paragraph indents and a line between paragraphs when I format my books. I think it gives them a better look. There are no hard and fast rules. If you have a large book you may want to use paragraph indents with no space between paragraphs to save on printing costs.

Create Space offers a variety of downloadable templates you can use to format your book. Just copy and paste your content in the appropriate spots and you're good to go.

If you're using images in your book ensure they are all high resolution images (300 DPI). Low resolution images can sometimes appear blurry or grainy. Create Space will single them out later in the proofing process to give you an opportunity to ensure they reproduce well.

If you follow these steps, you will have a good basic manuscript you can upload to Create Space. It should have no problems passing their automated system check. If you want your book to have a more professional look similar to a traditionally published book I would suggest hiring a professional formatter. They will ensure all of your chapters begin on the right hand page, and all of your front and back matter are professionally formatted. I've had good luck using sarahellestudio on Fiverr. For fifteen bucks she will format your book, add page numbers, headers, and drop caps to the first paragraph in each chapter. Here is the link to her formatting gig.

http://www.fiverr.com/sarahellestudio/format-your-manuscript-for-createspace

If you're a do-it-yourselfer check out *Self-Publishing: How to Publish like a Pro for a Fraction of the* Cost by Donna Joy Usher.

Getting Started with Create Space

Before you can start listing books on Create Space you need to register. Go to https://www.createspace.com/ and select *Sign up*.

Log into your account, click on *add new book* in your *member dashboard*. In the *Start your new project* box type in the name of your project, select *paperback*, and where it says choose a setup process select *guided* (especially for your first book). Press *get started* to move to the next screen.

Fill out the basic information for your book – title, author, contributors, etc. if you're unsure how to answer any questions, click on *what's this* and it will give you directions. At the bottom of the page, click save and continue.

Next you're asked to choose an ISBN. You have four choices.

1. Most authors choose to have Create Space assign a free ISBN for their book.

2. You can purchase a custom ISBN from Create Space for ten dollars. If you have your own publishing company or

imprint this is an inexpensive way to add a more professional look to your book.

3. You can purchase a custom universal ISBN from Create Space for $99. This gives you more options than the generic ISBN. The difference is you can use the custom universal ISBN with other publishers, whereas if you purchase the regular custom ISBN it can only be used through Create Space.

4. The final option is to provide your own ISBN. You can buy them through Bowker, or from online discounters.

Depending on the type of ISBN you purchase it can limit some of your distribution options. Any of them can be used with expanded distribution to help you sell more books. If you want to sell your books through libraries and educational institutions you need to use a Create Space assigned ISBN.

Select the option you want, and follow the prompts for it. Click on *assign ISBN* to move to the next section. The next page you see shows you your ten digit and thirteen digit ISBN. A message pops up to tell you your ISBN is locked, and cannot be changed. If you want to change the title or author you need to assign your book a new ISBN.

Click on continue.

This section lets you select the trim size and interior of your book. The default trim size is 6 inches x 9 inches. If your book is a different size, select *choose a different size*, and pick the size you want to use. After this you need to choose an interior type – black and white or colored pages. Choose your page style – cream or white. Cream pages more closely resemble the look of a traditional book. It may just be me, but I think the white pages look cheesy and unprofessional. Once you've made a choice, you're locked in and unable to change it later.

The next section lets you upload your book file. Choose *upload your book file*, and you will be prompted to choose a file. Manuscripts are accepted in these file formats -- .pdf, .doc, .docx, and .rtf. You're also offered the option of talking with someone from Create Space about professional design services. Costs start at $199 depending upon the amount of formatting involved. Don't waste your money on Create Space formatting, a formatter on Fiverr will do the same job for way less money.

While you're waiting for the interior file to upload and go through the automated print check you have the option to *start working on your book cover while you wait*, otherwise it takes a few minutes to process. When the automated print check is finished it will let you know if any errors were found. Click on *launch interior reviewer* to proof the contents of your book. You can page through your book and see what the final printing will look like.

When you're proofing your book, pay special attention to your formatting and page breaks. A lot of times when you format your book for Kindle, Word inserts a blank page when you add a page break. You need to ensure you remove all of the blank pages when you format your print version, or it's going to look strange having random blank pages. You also want to watch for orphan text, where you have just one or two lines of text on the last page of a chapter. You may want to tighten up your writing or remove spaces to avoid this.

Once you're sure everything looks good, click on *continue*.

This section lets you work on your cover. Select a finish for your cover. The choices are matte or glossy. Matte is a dull finish. Glossy is bright and shiny. For my money the matte finish makes a better looking book. After you've selected your cover, choose how you want to submit your cover design. You have three options for this.

1. Use the Create Space cover creator.
2. Hire a professional cover designer from Create Space (starting at $399).
3. Upload a PDF ready cover.

I'm not going to go into details on the Create Space cover designer. You can give it a shot, and see what you can turn out. Some of the styles are nice. It all comes down to whether you want to put a generic cover on your book.

I would suggest hiring your own professional designer. There are several designers on Fiverr who do a good job, and will format your Create Space cover for ten to twenty dollars. Two of them I've had good luck working with are –

http://www.fiverr.com/rroxx/create-awesome-professional-ebook-cover-design

http://www.fiverr.com/vikncharlie/design-you-an-awesome-book-cover

If you're uploading your own book cover select browse to choose your file, and click on *save*. The next page shows your cover has been successfully uploaded. It also gives you the option to *make changes*. If you're happy with what you have click on *continue*.

Next, submit your book for review. Before you submit your files you're given the option to edit files. If everything looks good select *submit files for review*. A pop up box appears telling you your files are being checked. Click on *continue* to select your distribution options.

Your books are automatically listed for sale on Amazon.com, Amazon Europe, and in the Create Space eStore. Royalties are larger when you sell through the Create Space eStore, so wherever possible link to it when you're selling copies of your own book from your website or blog.

The next section shows you the expanded distribution options. You can choose one, or all of these, depending upon how you want to make your book available.

Selecting *Bookstores and online retailers* makes your book available through online retailers. It takes about four to eight weeks for them to start selling on other sites, but when they finally show up your books will be available on Barnes & Noble, Books A Million, eBay, and others. You make less in royalties on each sale when they are sold through expanded distribution but you have the opportunity to reach more readers. In my case, I make between $250 and $300 per month from expanded distribution sales. Odds are they're sales I wouldn't have made otherwise, so I consider it free money.

The *Libraries and Academic institutions* option lets you sell your books to schools and libraries. *Create Space Direct* makes your books available through independent bookstores and retailers. You're book isn't likely to appear on store shelves, but if customers request it a bookstore can order a copy for them.

After you've selected your distribution channels, click on save and continue.

Now you can set your prices.

Create Space shows you a minimum price (you must charge at least this much for each book). Before you set your price play with the pricing tool and see what you will earn at different price points. If you selected expanded distribution, make sure you won't be losing money if you price your book too low. From what I understand Create Space will deduct any losses from your royalties.

If you write fiction a good price is probably somewhere between $7.99 and $12.99 depending upon what other books in your genre are selling for. If your book is nonfiction you should be able to ask a higher price. I charge $15.99 for most of my eBay guidebooks. One of them sells a consistent one hundred copies per month. Several others sell twenty-five to fifty copies per month. I've seen other authors stretch their price to $19.99, or $25.99. The nice thing is you can change your prices at any time.

Understand if your book is enrolled in expanded distribution it can sometimes take two to three months for the price to go back up.

When you're done pricing your book, click on *save and continue*.

The final step is to set up your book description, categories, author bio and such. You're allowed to use a maximum of 4,000 characters in your description. You can use basic HTML to enhance your description – bold, italic, list, etc. To add a space between lines you need to add the <br> code. To add a space between paragraphs use

.

You're only allowed to choose one category so pick the one that best defines your book. Under *additional information* you can add your author bio. I copy and paste it from my Amazon Author page. Be sure to use HTML code to dress it up. Add the <br> code to add spacing between lines and paragraphs. Under search keywords you're able to enter five search terms. I believe the maximum character length is twenty-five, so keep that in mind when you are entering them. When you are finished with this section, click on *save and continue*.

At this point you're done entering your book information. You need to wait twelve to twenty-four hours for Amazon to check your files. When Create Space completes their automated file check they will email you with the results. If everything is okay you will be asked to proof your book. You can use the online proofer, download a PDF proof, or order a physical proof of your book.

Once you approve your proof your book will go live on Amazon. Most times Amazon will automatically associate your print book with your eBook. If they haven't done it after three days, email customer service and they will get it taken care of for you. Alternately, you can email customer service as soon as your book is published and it will be tied to your Kindle book sooner.

. . . .

When you're finished setting up your Create Space book you're offered the option to have your book formatted and sold on Kindle. My suggestion is not to do this. If you formatted your book using Microsoft Word, it's notorious for adding extra characters to a manuscript. If you're like me, you probably added some extra line spaces here and there to make your book look better for print.

When Create Space translates your manuscript for Kindle the finished product isn't going to be pretty. Chances are it's going to be hard to read, and cause you to get some really bad reviews.

Best advice. Format your Kindle book yourself, and ensure it's done properly.

. . . .

Overall I've had a great experience using Create Space. My royalties per book are two to three times what I make selling a Kindle book and the best news is they pay royalties thirty days after they're earned.

FYI: Most times Amazon will discount your books by a few bucks to keep sales rolling in. The nice thing is, even when they discount the retail price of your book, they pay you royalties based on the full retail price.

It works the same way if another retailer drops their price, and Amazon lowers their price to match them. I had this happen with one of my books. Normal price was $12.99. Barnes & Noble dropped their price to $7.99 and Amazon matched it. I still received $5.62 in royalties per copy. The only exception was on copies sold through expanded distribution. My royalties for those sales were based on the $7.99 retail.

If you don't have a paperback version of your book I would encourage you to get one made.

Audible (ACX)

ACX is an Amazon company that sells books in the audio book format. They make audio books available on Audible, Amazon, and iTunes.

The least you need to know is audio books are still an emerging market. Compared to Amazon's twenty-five million plus titles, Audible has just 150,000 audio books available. Over the next five years that number is expected to grow to over one million audio books. That puts audio books in the same position Kindle was in three or four years ago. Audio books are a growth market, and there's plenty of opportunity for good books, producers, and narrators.

Getting started on ACX is easy for authors.

Visit ACX.com. Midway down the page you will see an address bar that asks you to enter your ISBN, book title, or author name. After you do this ACX will display your book, or a list of your books. To get started click on the *This is my book tab*, and you will be taken to the next step in the process.

Select how you want to make your book available.

The choices are:

1. I'm looking for someone to narrate and produce my audio book.
2. I have this book in audio and I want to sell it.
3. I will narrate my own book and upload it later.

The first option is what most authors should select. It will help you to find a qualified narrator to read and produce your book. When you select this option ACX shows you their book posting agreement. To proceed to the next step you need to read it over and click *Agree & Continue.*

On the next page you're asked to fill in some general information about your book, and who it is directed at. The book description is prepopulated for you with the information from your Amazon book page. Where it asks for copyright information normally you are the copyright owner for the book and for the audio book. Fill this information in along with the year of copyright.

You're asked if your book is fiction or nonfiction. Then you're asked to select the one category that best describes your book.

Below that you need to answer some general questions about the ideal narrator's voice you're looking for. Try to be as specific as possible when you're filling this section out. It will save you from listening to a lot of auditions that totally miss the mark on what you want.

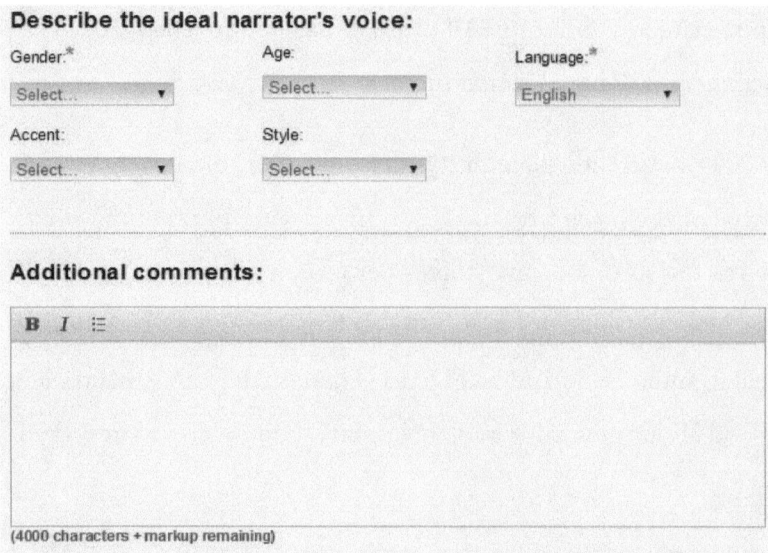

Describe the ideal narrator's voice:

Gender:*   Age: Language:*

Select... ▼   Select... ▼   English ▼

Accent: Style:

Select... ▼   Select... ▼

Additional comments:

B *I* ☰

(4000 characters + markup remaining)

Here's your chance to provide directions or advice to Producers who may audition for this book. It is also a good place to make your book as appealing as possible to ACX Producers. For example, you can include marketing information, selling points, best-seller status, awards, foreign language translations and reviews. Additionally, please include information about the Author's reach and fan-base (i.e. 5,000 followers on Twitter, 8,000 fans on

Use the *additional comments* section to list more information about your book, or about what you are looking for in a narrator. When I list my books I talk about their ranking on Amazon, how many books I am selling monthly and weekly, and how I am promoting them. Producers tell me this information helps them decide if the project will pay off for them or not.

I considered a few of my books marginal, meaning they were only selling a few copies a month in Kindle or paperback. I let producers know that, and explained to them the books were short, easy to produce, and while they might not make a lot of money on the project it could be fun. I think producers appreciated my honesty. All of my projects were snapped up within a few days of listing them.

I currently have thirty-six books available through ACX. Some of them sell fifty to seventy-five copies per month; others sell as few as one or two copies per month. What's funny is you can have a book that barely sells on Kindle become your best-selling audio book and vice-versa. There's really no explaining it. It's all about how your audience wants their information served up.

The last step on this page is to upload your audition script. You can upload a file, or link to a URL where you have the audition script located. ACX doesn't give you a character length to use as a guideline. I generally upload three to five pages of text. Don't just choose the first few pages of your manuscript. If your book is fiction, make sure the section you upload has two or three different character voices so you can see how the narrator approaches them. If your book is nonfiction, include a section with quotes, to see how they voice them.

Some voice actors have a repertoire of character voices they can use in your book; others just read the lines and don't worry about character voices. Some producers have a team of voice actors so they have separate men's and women's voices. Decide for yourself what sounds best for your book.

After you've uploaded your sample click ok at the bottom of the page and you will be directed to the final page of information ACX needs to collect.

At the top of this page you're asked to type in how many words are in your book. When you do this they estimate how many hours your final production will be.

Where it asks for territory rights put in the regions you hold the copyright for. The default response is world. If you only hold rights for one country or territory list that location instead.

The next section lets you choose how you want to pay for your production. There are two choices:

1. **Royalty share**. The narrator / producer covers the entire cost of production, and does all of the work associated with it. When the audio book goes up for sale you split royalties 50 / 50 with them. ACX handles all of the details and pays each of you separately. Your only responsibility is to upload a book cover (2500 x 2500 pixels).

2. **Pay for production**. You pay a narrator /producer to make the audio book for you, and in return you receive all royalties earned from sales of your audio book. If you choose this option you can enter the amount you are willing to pay per hour of finished audio. The going rate is $200 to $400 per finished hour, although I have seen some producers offering to work for as little as $50 per hour, and others listing their rates at $500 or more per finished hour.

After you select your payment method you are prompted to select the type of distribution you want. If you selected royalty share your only option is exclusive distribution through Audible,

Amazon, and iTunes. Your royalty is 40%, and it is split 50 / 50 between you and the producer.

If you paid for the production of your audio book you can choose non-exclusive distribution. This lets you sell through Audible, Amazon, iTunes, and other methods of your choice. Your royalty this way is 25% and you keep all of it.

After you've made these selections, click *Save & Continue* to move to the final page. This page summarizes your information and gives you the option to post your information to ACX.

If you already have the book on audio and want to distribute it through ACX, chose the second option – *I have this book in audio and want to sell it.* Follow the prompts to list your book through ACX. You need to choose the territory you have rights for, select exclusive distribution through ACX (40% royalty), or non-exclusive (25% royalty). After you do this, you move to the next page and agree to ACX's terms of service. The final page allows you to give information about your book, and post it for sale.

The last option is to record your own audio and upload your book yourself. If you choose to do this ACX offers a number of tips on how to do the best job possible. You may also want to check out *How to Create an Audiobook for Audible* by Rob

Archangel and Buck Flogging. They explain the process in more detail and talk about the equipment you need to make a good recording.

....

My experience with ACX has been amazing. Their interface is easy to use. You are prompted to include the proper information every step of the way so it's unlikely you will mess anything up. Within hours of posting my books, I received dozens of auditions, many of them from producers with years of experience doing voiceover work and narrating eBooks. My first four books were ready and up for sale in less than three weeks. The first week my audio books were up for sale we sold fifty-eight copies.

The key to getting good results is to carefully listen to each of your auditions. Ask yourself if the narrator's voice and tone matches your book. Most often I know within the first ten seconds of listening to the audition if the narrator is a good fit for my book. Trust your gut. If it sounds good to you, it will probably sound good to other listeners.

Finally, be open to new ideas.

I wrote some short erotica, and somehow got it in my head that it required a male voice to narrate it. I received an email out of the blue from a girl asking if I was set on a male narrator. I thought about it for a while and told her to shoot me an audition. She did, and it was exactly what I was looking for (even though I didn't know it at the time). She had the exact voice and tone needed to bring the story to life.

So before you say no, or set your specifications, make sure you know what you really want. And, be open to new ideas.

If you're not sure about a narrator, pass on the audition. There are plenty of producers and narrators looking for good projects and they will find your book if you give them time.

. . . .

Final thought. I listed twenty-three audio books for production in the same week. As a result I went with the royalty share option on all of them. It saved me money up front, and it allowed me to get all the projects going at the same time. If I had it to do again, I would cherry pick my books, and pay for the production of my bestsellers up front. Over the long haul I would probably make thousands of dollars more in royalties.

. . . .

ACX pays royalties a month after they are earned, so the money begins flowing in quickly. Payments are deposited directly into your bank account, and they mail out a printed earnings statement a week or two after royalties are paid out.

Title ▲	Author	On Sale Date	Sales data AL (units)	ALOP (units)	ALC (units)	Total Sales (units)	Additional earnings Bounty (units)
7 Steps to a New Job, What Employers Are Really Looking for in Today's Troubled Economy (Unabridged) Title on Audible | Title on ACX	Nick Vulich	4/16/14	0	10	9	19	0
Abraham Lincoln: The Baltimore Plot (Unabridged) Title on Audible | Title on ACX	Nicholas L. Vulich	4/29/14	2	0	1	3	0
Banging Your Way Across Craigslist: How to Pick-up, Flirt, Seduce, and Sleep with Women on Craigslist (Unabridged) Title on Audible | Title on ACX	Braun Schweiger	4/17/14	3	9	5	17	0
Fit After Fifty: How to Lose Weight, Get Fit, and Stay Fit for Life (Unabridged) Title on Audible | Title on ACX	Nick Vulich	4/25/14	3	8	1	12	0
Freaking Idiots Guide Two-Book Bundle: eBay Unleashed and Freaking Idiots Guide to Selling on eBay (Unabridged)	Nick Vulich	5/6/14	9	12	2	23	0
Totals Based on date range of 01/01/2011 - 06/06/2014			137	230	116	483	2

They pay a bounty on each book you sell that brings in a new subscriber. Bounties are $50 for the first purchase made by an Audible listener member. The qualifier is they must remain members for a minimum of sixty-one days. If your book is on a royalty share deal you receive $25, and the producer of your book receives $25 for each bounty paid out.

I'm currently getting one bounty for roughly every 100 sales. So that works out to between three and four bounty payments per month. As time goes on, hopefully that number will go up.

Audible has another unadvertised program to help boost your sales. They've sent me twenty-five free download codes for several of my books with a suggestion that you raffle them off on your website, blog, etc. to draw new readers. From my understanding you receive royalties for each book downloaded with the free code, and receive a bounty if the purchase is eligible for one.

The downside to passing out free download coupons is if recipients aren't current Audible members, they are required to sign up for the service to claim your free book. In a few cases this has created problems when I gave the audio books away, so you may want to tell people the terms of the giveaway before you ask them to sign up.

Babelcube

Babelcube connects writers with translators.

It's easy to use. Just post your profile, upload information about your books, and wait for independent translators to contact you. For authors, there's no cost up front. Babelcube handles all of the details and splits the profits between you, the translator, and of course, they keep a small cut for the house.

Commissions are based on how much revenue your books take in. Babelcube takes 15% for brokering the deal. Your split ranges from 30% to 75% depending upon how many copies your book sells and the revenue generated. You receive 30% of revenues for sales under $2,000, and 75% for sales over $8,000. Similar to Amazon, they pay sixty days after sales are made. One caveat, your payment needs to be $50.00 or greater to receive a payment for the month. To view the complete royalty schedule follow this link http://www.babelcube.com/faq/revenue-share.

I've inked deals to have eight of my eBay books translated into Spanish, Italian, and French by six different translators.

My personal thought is Babelcube is a great concept. They recently updated their user interface, but it's still hard to work with.

. . . .

To get started you need to sign up at http://www.babelcube.com/register/.

At the top of your home page there are four tabs – profile, books, translations, and messages.

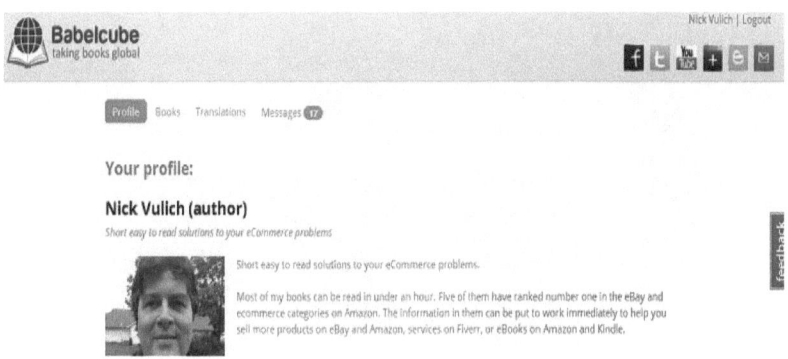

When you click on Profile you're asked to provide all of your contact information. Fill in as much as you can. I posted my Amazon author bio, my picture, and included links to my website.

When you click on the Books section it gives you the option to Add Books. Follow the prompts and add your book details. I copied my book description and most of the other information from my Amazon book page. You can add just one book, or your entire catalog.

Add a book
Please provide all you book details, including information about sales, ranks and anything that could make this book an atractive proposition to translators
If you want, you can provide a sample text from the book so that translators can evaluate the book style and submit test translations.

Title: *

Author: *

Cover Image: *
Choose File | No file chosen
One line description: *

The Translations tab shows what offers you have received to translate your books, and a list of the translations you have in progress. Click on the book title and scroll down to the bottom of the page to get more information about your projects. This section shows a list of translations you have in progress, and names of the translators handling the project. At the bottom of the page there are three tabs – edit book, upload book material, and return.

Edit book lets you change your book description or upload a new cover. Upload book material lets you upload your book file, book description, and an author biography. Your translator will also translate your biography and book description when they prepare the book for publication. When you press Return it takes you back to your profile page.

The Messages tab holds all of your correspondence so you can send messages to your translators, and correspond back and forth with people wanting to translate your books.

. . . .

Babelcube will email you when you receive an offer to translate your book. You can check out the offer by logging into your Babelcube account and selecting translations.

The translations page is divided into two sections – Offers to translate your books, and books being translated.

All of your current offers will be grouped in the offers to translate your book section. Click on the offer details in the status column. It will contain a sample of translated text, and information on how soon the translator will complete your project. The first date shown is when you can expect the first ten pages of the project. The second date is the expected completion date when your entire book will be translated.

Offers to translate your books:

Book Title	Translator(s)	Translate into	Status
Killing the Presidents Preside...	Victoria Day	Spanish	Canceled
eBay Unleashed, A beginners ...	Priyanka Nabar	French	Pending
			⬔ View offer
eBay Unleashed, A beginners ...	Madhura Oak	French	Pending
			⬔ View offer

Books being translated:

Book Title	Translator(s)	Translate into	Status
eBay Unleashed, A beginners ...	Miguel Segura	Spanish	Finished
			☰ Publishing status
			✎ Book sales
			⬔ Republish book

Most of the translators I've worked with offer to deliver the first ten pages within five to ten days, and the completed translation within twenty to forty-five days.

When you receive the first ten pages look the translation over if you are familiar with the language. If you're not familiar with the language, ask a friend, a university professor, or someone familiar with the language to give it a once over to make sure everything sounds ok.

If everything is good, click the accept translation button to approve the translation.

At this point, I make a note of the title in the translated document and verify with the translator that this is the title they want to go with. After we've approved this I get with my cover designer to have the new cover made. In nine out of ten cases it's a simple matter of swapping out the title, and leaving the basic design the same.

You'll receive another email from Babelcube when the translation is completed.

To approve the final translation, return to the translations page. This time you're going to look for your book in the books being translated section. Click on the publish tab in the status column, and it will walk you through getting your book set up for publication.

Publishing your book on Babelcube is a four step process that should take less than five minutes.

1. Upload your translated book cover. To upload your new cover click on the choose file box, and select your cover file. Ensure your name, and the name of your cover designer is correct.

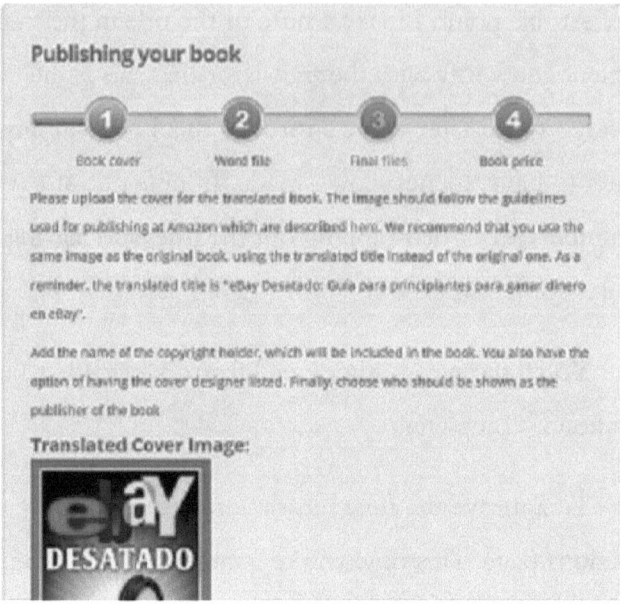

2. Check the word file. The translated word file is preloaded into the system by Babelcube. You can download a copy to your computer by selecting here, right after where it says download the file. As long as the first ten pages check out ok, I normally skip reviewing the entire document, and just assume everything is ok. If you make changes to the file, upload the revised document where it allows you to choose the new file to upload. Select next step at the bottom of the page to proceed to the next section.

3. Review the final document. Check the *I have reviewed this manuscript* box to approve the document, and select next step to proceed to the final section.

4. Set your book price. Babelcube lets you set the price of your book between 99¢ and $39.99. For best results they suggest you price your book between $2.99 and $9.99, which is in line with Amazon's sweet spot for pricing.

At this point your book is set to go, and should start publishing to Babelcube's partner sites within a few days. In my experience your books will show up on Kobo first, then Barnes and Noble. Amazon is normally the last site your book will show up on. Apple is iffy at best.

If you want your books to show up in the iStore you need to prepare your manuscript properly before you forward it to your translator. Remove all links to books on other book sites such as Amazon and Barnes & Noble. Make sure not to refer readers to check out any books on competing retailer websites, and if you ask readers to leave a review when they are finished reading, remove any references to specific book sites.

I include email links in most of my books so readers have a way to get ahold of me should they have any questions. Most times I have to remove my email address to get the book approved for the iStore. It's another one of Apple's idiosyncrasies.

If there are any complications, Babelcube will email to let you know that changes to your manuscript are required. Trust me it's easier to take care of these details when the manuscript is in your native language. I've had to look for problem areas in two translated documents and it's not fun.

. . . .

FYI: If you need to make changes, download a copy of the document in step two of the publish process. Make any necessary changes, then upload the new file where it says upload file in this step. Continue through the publishing process to complete your changes.

If you decide you want to change your prices go to the translations page, select republish translation, and go to step three. Enter your new price, and continue to the next step to publish your document.

. . . .

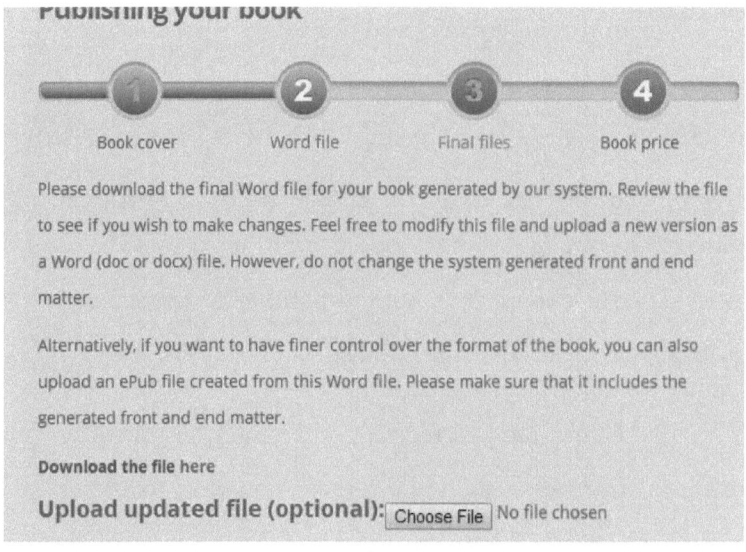

Final thoughts - I currently have eight books published through Babelcube. I have one more translation in the works. Not everything has gone smoothly. I had once translator working on three projects skip out on me, a few translators have missed their deadline by a day or two, but otherwise I think Babelcube is a decent site. Their customer service is top notch, and they normally answer questions within twenty-four hours.

For authors, there is very little downside. You can reach an entirely new audience with very little risk. Your only outlay is for a new cover, and that can be as little as five dollars if you use a designer from Fiverr.

From my experience, and the offers I have received to translate my books, the majority of translators on the site work with Spanish, Italian, French, and Portuguese. I haven't received any offers to translate my books into German, Japanese, or Chinese. I'm not sure if that's because of the types of books I write, or because there are a limited number of translators working with these languages on Babelcube.

Babelcube did just recently add a sales dashboard so you can check your sales results. To go to it you need to visit your *translations* tab. To the far right of each book you will see three tabs. Choose *book sales* to see your results.

Another new feature is the *Royalties* tab.

When you click on the Royalties tab you can update your tax and payment information, download monthly sales reports, download monthly royalty payment reports, or scroll down to the bottom of the page to get a quick look at the balance in your royalty account. Remember Babelcube does not pay out until your royalties total fifty dollars.

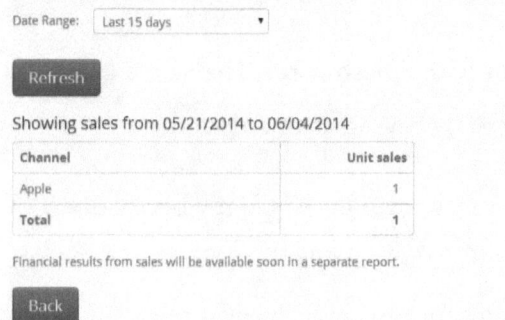

Book sales of translation of "Sell it Online: How to Make Money Selling on eBay, Amazon, Fiverr & Etsy" into Spanish

Date Range: Last 15 days ▾

Refresh

Showing sales from 05/21/2014 to 06/04/2014

Channel	Unit sales
Apple	1
Total	1

Financial results from sales will be available soon in a separate report.

Back

Babelcube has been growing quickly, and they appear to be adding new selections to the website every few weeks. Over time they could become a major force in e-publishing.

Smashwords

I have a love hate affair with Smashwords. Here's the link to visit their website - https://www.smashwords.com/.

I'm happy for the opportunity to get my books on all of the sites they support, but I can't for the life of me figure out how to configure a manuscript to get it through their "meatgrinder." The good news is I don't have to.

After a week of pulling out my hair and fighting urges to smash my laptop against the wall I found a guy on Fiverr who'll do all the work for me for five bucks. His Fiverr id is Bookaholic, and he does the job in three days or less. If you want to check out his gig here's the link.

http://www.fiverr.com/bookaholic/format-your-ebook-for-smashwords-to-pass-autovetter.

Here's the least you need to know about Smashwords. They're a third party aggregator that posts content on their own website, and on other eBook sites. Some of the sites they make your books available on include:

- Amazon
- Apple
- Baker & Taylor Blio

46

- Baker-Taylor Axis 360

- Barnes & Noble

- Flipkart

- Kobo

- Library Direct

- Oyster

- Page Foundry

- Scribd

The big three are Apple, Kobo, and Barnes & Noble.

Apple is the toughest nut for independent authors to crack on their own because Apple requires you to use their own eBook authoring software that only runs on – you guessed it – an Apple computer.

Publishing your book

Smashwords does all of the heavy lifting for you. When you submit a manuscript to them it gets run through their "meatgrinder." This is what converts your manuscript into all the different formats they need to publish your book on other sites. In order to do this they have very specific guidelines your manuscript needs to conform to.

For the sake of my own sanity and this book I'm not going to cover their exact requirements. I suggest using the Fiverr gig by Bookaholic. If you want to go it on your own you should check out the *Smashwords Style Guide* by Mark Coker. You can get your free copy here.

http://www.smashwords.com/books/view/52.

Your cover art may also need some minor tweaking to work with Smashwords. They require your cover to be a minimum of 1400 pixels wide, with a height greater than the width. You can resize your cover using paint, or ask your designer to redo it for you.

. . . .

Once you have your manuscript and cover ready publishing on Smashwords is easy. Click on *publish* in the author dashboard. Most everything is self-explanatory.

The pricing and sampling section is different than on Amazon. You have the option to make your book permanently free on Smashwords. To do this select *make my book free*. Authors generally do this when they want to make their book permanently free on Amazon or other eBook sites. You're also given the option to *let my readers determine the price.* If you're feeling lucky give this one a try. Readers can pay whatever they think your book is worth. Keep in mind, if you use this option, Barnes and Noble won't publish your book if you submit it through Smashwords. The final option is *charge a specific price for my book.* Use this section to set the price you want for your book.

Publish Your Book

Authors and publishers — quick checklist before you proceed.
1. **Do not** upload your book until you have implemented the recommendations in **The Smashwords Style Guide**. Smashwords reserves the right to remove poorly formatted books.
2. **Do not** use this page to publish an updated version of a previously uploaded book. Instead, go to your **Dashboard** and click "Upload a new version."
3. **Do not** upload a book unless you are the original author or exclusive publisher. No public-domain or private-label-rights books.

1   Title and synopsis

Title

The title of your book (up to 250 characters).

Release date

Smashwords is shipping preorders to Apple, Barnes & Noble, and Kobo. Learn the benefits of preorders.

⦿ For immediate release (will publish to the Smashwords store in minutes).

◯ Make it a preorder—schedule release date in the future. (Visit our preorder help page before you select this option!)

Synopsis

The section immediately after this lets you to set up sampling. Amazon automatically sets sampling or the *look inside* feature to ten percent. Smashwords lets you select the sample size for your book. Twenty percent is the default setting. They suggest fifteen percent for full size books and thirty percent for short stories. Choose the preview amount you're comfortable giving away.

Section 5 lets you select the eBook formats to make your book available in. By default all of the formats are selected. My suggestion is to leave it like that.

After you've completed all of the steps, select *yes, I agree* in Section 8 and Smashwords will begin to process your book.

Once you select *yes, I agree* your book goes into a queue waiting to be processed. When processing is completed you receive an email saying congratulations your book passed the vetting process, or you will receive a message that your book had issues going through the autovetter. If you had autovetter issues you can correct them, and resubmit your manuscript.

As soon as you receive the congratulations message your book goes on sale on the Smashwords site. It also goes into review for premium distribution, which means it is good to be sold on other sites like Apple, Kobo, and Scribd. Most often it takes about a week to review your book and get it set up for premium distribution.

You can check the progress in your dashboard. The second to the last column at the far right of each book summary shows the premium status. When your book has been accepted it will show *premium approved*, and the date of approval. If there is an issue getting approved, you will be able to see the error code in the next column – *retailer tickets*. As soon as you correct the error you can resubmit your book.

Book Summaries

Title	Status	Operations	Retail Price	Library Price	Books Sold	Full & Sample Downloads	In User Libraries	Date Published	Premium Status	Retailer Tickets
eBay Selling Explained How to take your eBay Sales to an all New Level	Published unpublish	Settings | Upload new version | Coupon | Stats | SEO |	$5.99 USD	$5.99 USD via retail price	1	Click to sort by Books Sold		2014-01-08	✓ Premium approved 2014-05-30	View closed tickets
Make Money Online: Step-by-Step Directions How I Make $2500 a Month Selling on eBay, Fiverr, Amazon & More	Published unpublish	Settings | Upload new version | Coupon | Stats | SEO |	$3.99 USD	$3.99 USD via retail price	0	67 (details)	1	2014-01-12	✓ Premium approved 2014-01-22	No tickets
Fit After Fifty: How to Lose Weight, Get Fit, and Stay Fit For Life	Published unpublish	Settings | Upload new version | Coupon | Stats | SEO |	$2.99 USD	$2.99 USD via retail price	0	55 (details)	1	2014-01-15	✓ Premium approved 2014-04-10	No tickets
eBay Subject Matter Expert: 5 Weeks to Becoming an eBay Subject Matter Expert	Published unpublish	Settings | Upload new version | Coupon | Stats | SEO |	$2.99 USD	$2.99 USD via retail price	0	48 (details)	0	2014-01-18	✓ Premium approved 2014-05-28	No tickets

Selecting distribution channels

After you submit your book you have one last task to complete, you need to select your distribution channels. To do this select *channel manager* in the box labeled *Marketing & Distribution Tools*.

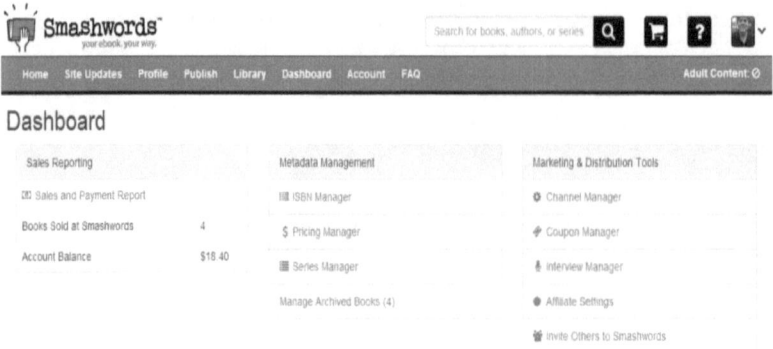

When you click into the channel manager the first thing you see is an explanation of the royalties paid selling your book on the different sites. To select your sales channels scroll further down the page until you see your first book cover. Smashwords shows you the different channels available and gives you the option to *Distribute* or *Opt Out* of each channel.

I list my books on Amazon, Barnes & Noble, and Kobo for myself so I choose to opt out of those three programs. This way I receive payment directly from these sites, and don't have to pay a commission on those sales to Smashwords. Others authors prefer the convenience of doing it all through Smashwords and just having one distributor. You can always change your distribution options later, if you decide to publish to those channels on your own. I did this with Kobo when I discovered how easy it was to use their *Writing Life* interface.

After you've selected your channels to sell on it normally takes anywhere from one to four weeks for your books to start selling on those sites.

Sony	Barnes & Noble	Kobo	Amazon	Apple	Diesel	Page Foundry	Baker & Taylor Blio	txtr	Library Direct
Not currently shipped	Opt-out requested on 2014-02-12. Will not ship	Opt-out requested on 2014-05-12 Will not ship	Opt-out requested on 2014-02-12 Will not ship.	2014-02-12 revision shipped on 2014-05-28.	2014-02-12 revision shipped on 2014-02-26. Will ship 2014-05-25 revision	2014-02-12 revision shipped on 2014-05-28.	2014-02-12 revision shipped on 2014-05-29	2014-02-12 revision shipped on 2014-06-06.	This title is available for purchase by libraries directly via Smashwords.
Will be shipped.									
● Distribute				● Distribute		● Distribute	● Distribute	● Distribute	
○ Opt out	○ Distribute ● Opt out	○ Distribute ● Opt out	○ Distribute ● Opt out	○ Opt out	● Distribute ○ Opt out	○ Opt out	○ Opt out	○ Opt out	● Distribute ○ Opt out

As expected, Apple is the most difficult vendor to work with.

When you format your manuscript make sure to remove all of the links to other eBook sites. I know I missed this step on several of my manuscripts. I usually include a clickable bibliography with links to where readers can find those books on Amazon or Google Books. That's a big no no with Apple, unless you change to links to books in the iStore.

Another area I've been caught with my pants down on was where I included a link to my book on Amazon to ask for a review. Apple will reject your book if you link to Amazon, or even if you just mention that readers should stop back to Amazon to ask for a review.

To make it easy on yourself thoroughly check your book for links to other eBook sites and remove all of them.

Payment

Payments are made quarterly on Smashwords. Authors can choose to receive payment by PayPal or check. The payment threshold for PayPal is $10.00, for checks the payment threshold is $75.00.

Books Sold

Smashwords.com (all-time): 4

Retailer	Sales in 2014
Amazon	0
Apple	21
Baker & Taylor Blio	1
Baker-Taylor Axis360	0
Barnes & Noble	0
Diesel	0
Flipkart	0
Kobo	0
Library Direct	0
OverDrive	0
Oyster	0
Page Foundry	0
Scribd	3
Sony	0

Payment dates are:

- January 31st (for sales in October, November, and December)
- April 30th (for sales in January, February, and March)
- July 31st (for sales in April, May, and June)
- October 31st (for sales in July, August, and September)
  To check out Smashwords FAQs click this link -

http://www.smashwords.com/about/supportfaq#Royalties.

New update to Sales Dashboard

One of the most frustrating things about selling on Smashwords was always the lag time between making a sale, and having it reported in your sales dashboard. It used to take a month or two before you knew if your books were selling.

Yesterday (06/11) they came out with a great new tool that gives you daily sales updates for iBooks, Kobo, Barnes & Noble, and Smashwords. You can find it at the top of your dashboard in the sales reporting box. Click on daily sales, and it will take you to the page shown below.

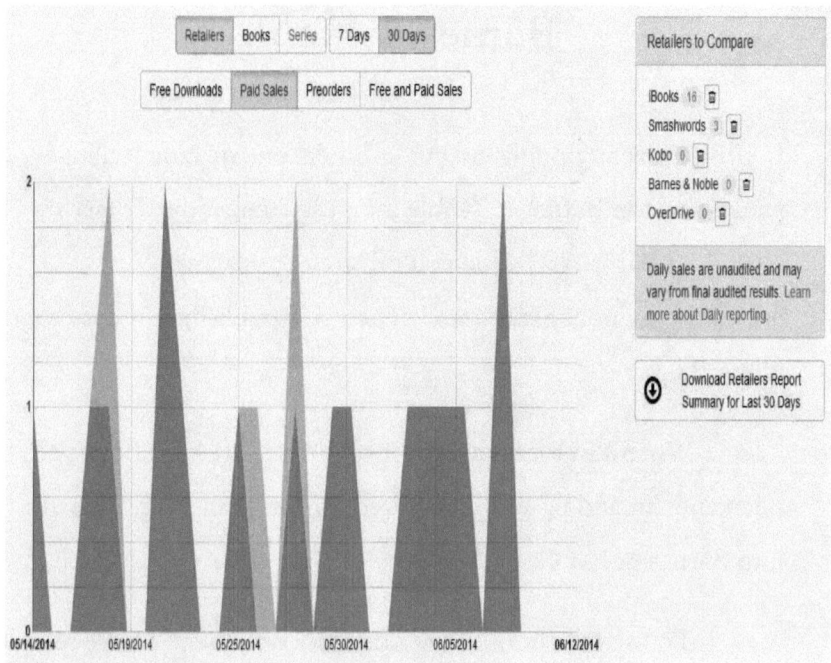

Smashwords new sales graph. You can click on each item to see just the books sold that day, or the books sold at each retailer.

Barnes & Noble

If you're already publishing your books on Amazon, selling your books on Barnes & Noble is an easy transition. To get started on Barnes & Noble you can follow this link https://www.nookpress.com/. Their self-publishing site is called Nook Press.

When I'm listing a new book I normally keep both sites open and cut and paste the required information from Amazon into Barnes & Noble.

To list your book, click on *Create new project*. You're asked to give your project a name. It can be the name of your book or another name you want to assign to it. The next screen asks you to upload your manuscript. You can use the same MS Word file you submitted to Amazon, just be sure to remove any references or links to Amazon in it.

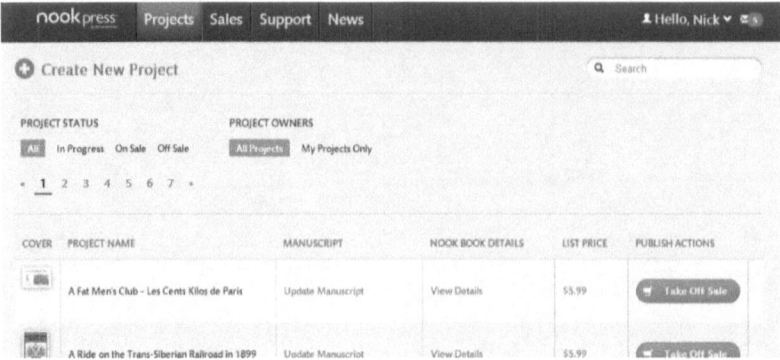

Once your manuscript has been uploaded, click on *cover image* to upload your book cover.

After your cover has been uploaded click on *title & description*. The first step is to update your title. Next you are given the option to include a publisher name. If you have your own imprint name put it here. If you don't have your own publisher name leave this item blank.

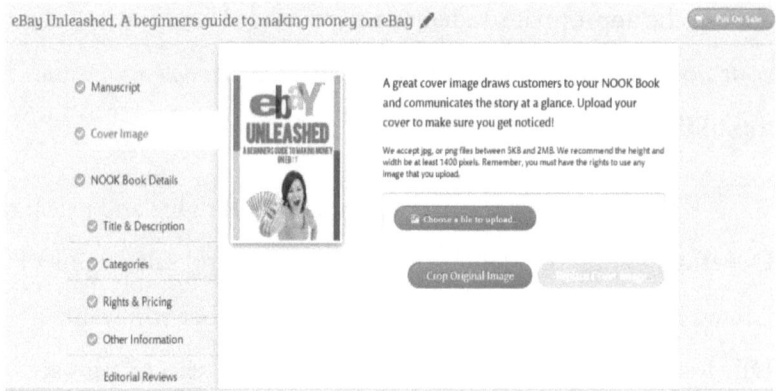

Use contributors *to* include anyone who participated in creating your book – authors, co-authors, editors, illustrators, etc. Below this is a section for your book description. I paste mine in directly from Amazon. The next section lets you enter your author bio. Once again, I paste it directly from Amazon. The last question asks if you have an eBook specific ISBN. In most cases your answer will be no, and they will assign a free ISBN for your book. Be sure to click *save and next* at the top before you proceed, or you may lose all of your information.

After this you add categories. Barnes & Noble lets you select up to five categories, compared to only two with Kindle. Use all five categories if possible. Below this you are asked to enter keywords readers can search on to find your book. You are allowed 100 characters, and should separate each search term with a comma. At the bottom of this section you are asked to choose the appropriate audience for your book and the language your book is written in. Once again click on *save and next* at the top of the page.

The next page asks for information on rights and pricing. Depending upon the rights you own select World sales rights or United States only. DRM lets you choose whether you want DRM encryption set up for your book. Finally, select your list price for the United States and the United Kingdom. When you are done entering this information click *save and next*.

The next section concerns book details. Answer these questions, and click on *save and next*.

The final section allows you to enter editorial reviews. If you have some enter them here. If not click on *save*, and the *publish* button will turn green at the top. Click on it, and your book is ready to be published. One more screen pops up and asks you which version of your manuscript to use. The one you edited in the previewer (if you changed anything), or the original version you uploaded.

After this, your book should be available for sale within eight to twelve hours.

. . . .

Royalties and Payments

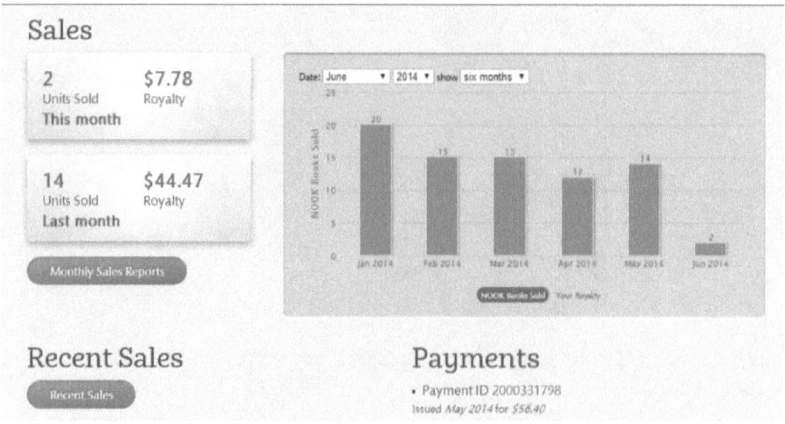

Barnes and Noble pay out royalties sixty days after they are earned. My experience is they are not as consistent with their payouts as Amazon. Some months the payment does not arrive until two or three days into the new month, so some months you won't receive a payment.

Royalties are 40 percent for books priced under $2.98 or over $10.00. Royalties are sixty-five percent for books priced between $2.99 and $9.99.

My experience with Barnes and Noble has been mixed. I normally receive a forty to fifty dollar royalty payment, compared to a thousand or more from Kindle. Part of that may be that my four bestselling books are exclusive to Amazon, so it's probably not a fair comparison.

Google Play & Google Books

Google Play and **Google Books** offer another platform for authors to sell their books on.

Google Books is the world's largest repository of out-of-print and current books. Readers can search through millions of books looking for information on a particular subject, and *Google Books* will show them the pages in your book that contain the search terms they are looking for. Every day readers, researchers, and authors turn to *Google Books* to find answers to their research questions.

Listing your works on *Google Books* can open it up to an entirely new audience.

Google Play is Google's version of Kindle or the iStore. They deliver books to readers who use their Android based platform. You can check out *Google Play* here https://play.google.com/store.

Getting started

To get started listing your books on Google go to
https://play.google.com/books/publish/. If you're not signed
up for the Google Partners Program you will need to sign up for
it first.

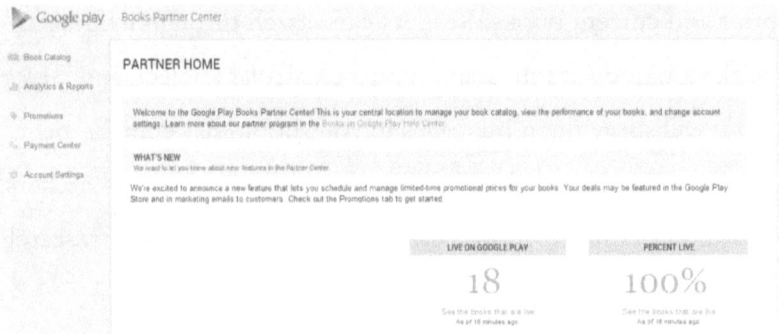

At the top of the browser page it says *Google Play* in the
upper left corner. Below that you will see four tabs – Book
Catalog, Analytics & Reports, Payment Center, and Account
Settings.

Book Catalog is where you add new books. Select the
Add Books tab, and follow the prompts. A pop up screen will ask
you for a book identifier (ISBN). Type in your book's ISBN. If it
doesn't have an ISBN click on the box below that. Click *ok*, and
you will be taken to the next screen.

If Google can locate your book in its database it prepopulates all of the screens with the information available. If Google doesn't find your book you will need to fill in all of the information. Where it asks for a biographical note, I paste in my Amazon author bio. Below that is a section labeled subjects. Use it to add categories for your book. Age groups lets you target different groups your book will appeal to. If the description doesn't prepopulate, copy and paste it from Amazon. When you are done filling in all of the info, click on *save* at the top of the page.

Click on *Google Play Settings* in the left hand column. The first thing you're asked is to add a new price. Click on Add a new price. Type in the currency your book is priced in (For example US Dollars is USD). In the next box you need to type in the price (example 3.99). Finally, you're asked to choose the location for that price. To make it easy, use "World." If you have different prices for different locations, you would need to add each of them separately. Follow through the rest of the prompts on this page. If you are unsure how to answer hover your mouse over the question mark and it will guide you through answering the question. Click on *save* at the top of the page.

Click on *Google Book Settings* in the left hand column. The first question asks you to select the preview type, or the percentage of your book you want to make available to readers. Twenty percent is the default, or you can choose another preview amount from twenty to one hundred percent. If you have the book available for sale directly from your website, fill in the buy link text and buy link, otherwise leave these lines blank. The publisher link is the link to your publisher website if you have one, otherwise leave this line blank. You can also upload a publisher logo if desired. Click on *save* at the top of the page.

Click on *Content Files* in the left hand column. This is where you upload your book files. Your book file needs to be uploaded in PDF or epub formats. The cover should be uploaded as a JPEG. At the bottom of this page you have the option to upload a list of Quality Reviewers. To add someone as a quality reviewer they must have a Google account. Click on add, and enter their email address. Click ok, and continue doing this to add more reviewers. When you are finished click the save button at the top of the page. Your quality reviewers will be able to access your book on their PCs or on their reading devices.

Reports / Payment Center / Account Settings

I want to briefly outline the other three selections you see under *Google Play* in the far left column of your screen.

ANALYTICS & REPORTS

Custom reports	CUSTOM REPORTS

Build your own reports by selecting from the query parameters below

Report type ⓘ   Google Play Sales Summary Report   ▾

See report for   ○ All time

           ◉ Date range   to

Pick countries   None   ▾

Export Complete Report

Analytics and reports lets you pull up reports regarding your book traffic and sales. The most irritating thing about Google is they don't provide a sales dashboard where you can quickly review your sales and earnings. Each time you want to check sales you need to generate a new report and download it as an Excel spreadsheet. Can you say irritating? Hopefully the folks at Google will figure this one out and make it more "user friendly."

The information in **payment center** needs to be completed before your books can go live on *Google Play* and

Google Books. To get started, click on the *payment center* tab. Click on *Add Payment profile.* Give your payment profile a name, and fill in the information asked for – name, address, etc.

The first thing you need to do is set up your payment settings. By default you are set up to receive monthly payments with a $1.00 payment threshold. You can change your payment threshold to another dollar amount, or you can have Google hold your payments for a specified period (up to one year). After you've completed this step, click on Add *new bank account.* Before you can finish setting up your bank account you need to wait for Google to make a test deposit to your account. When you see the deposit has been made to your account, click on *Add new bank account* again to verify the deposit amount.

Next you need to click on *billing profile.* Click on *edit*, and scroll down to *tax profile.* Enter your tax information in the online W9 form.

Scroll down to *sales territories.* Click on *add a territory.* Select a payment profile from the drop down menu. In the *choose territories* section most often you will type in "world." If you only hold rights in certain areas, click on the question mark and it will tell you how to set up individual territories. If you're subject to fixed pricing laws in any of the countries put a check mark in the box. If not, leave this box blank. Click on *enable this region configuration*, and select *create territory*.

The final section is **Account Settings**. Use it to ensure your contact information is correct, or to make any changes.

From signing up to verifying my account to listing my first books it took about seven days for my books to begin showing up in Google Play and Google Books.

Royalty rates and payments

I couldn't find any mention of royalties in the *Google Play* FAQs. When I searched for it in their help section it said there were no help pages for that topic. I don't know about anybody else, but that sort of scares me.

FYI: I sold my first book on *Google Play* three days after it went live. I set my list price at $4.99. Google discounted it to $3.60. They paid an after tax royalty based on a $3.00 selling price, so my royalty figured out to $1.56, or 52 percent.

Lesson learned: Add at least $2.00 to your selling price to ensure you receive the royalty you were expecting. The end result is I made fifty cents less than I would have received selling the same book for $2.99 on Amazon.

The good news is Google pays thirty days after sales are made, not sixty days like Amazon and Barnes and Noble so you will receive your payments sooner. I made six sales my first month. My second month I sold twelve books so I'm not going to strike it rich, but over time as I move my bestselling books out of Amazon exclusivity I expect these sales to pick up.

. . . .

One final word of caution. Google has been known to discount books at their own discretion, sometimes marking them down to free. The danger when they do this is Amazon will see your book posted for free. If they do, odds are they will match it, and list your book for free on Kindle. If this happens, you can pull your book out of the Play Store, but by the time you do, the damage will be done. It can take a week or more for Amazon to start charging for your book again. In the meantime, if Barnes & Noble discovers your book listed for free on either site, they could lower the price to free and the entire cycle could start over again.

This is one reason some authors refuse to publish their works in the Google Play Store.

Kobo

Kobo is the easiest to use self-publishing site I've come across. You can access the site by following this link.
http://www.kobo.com/writinglife

To read the Kobo user manual, click on this link.
http://download.kobobooks.com/writinglife/Kobo/en-US/KWL-User-Guide.pdf

. . . .

As soon as you sign into Kobo you will be taken to your seller dashboard. The dashboard is the money center of Kobo. It shows you how many eBooks you've sold, and your estimated earnings.

At the top of this page, just below where it says Kobo you'll see three tabs – dashboard, eBooks, and learning center. As we already talked about, dashboard highlights your sales and earnings. eBooks is where you set up new books for publication, and the learning center is where you can turn for more help in listing your books and increasing sales on Kobo.

. . . .

To list your first book with Kobo, click on eBooks at the top of the page.

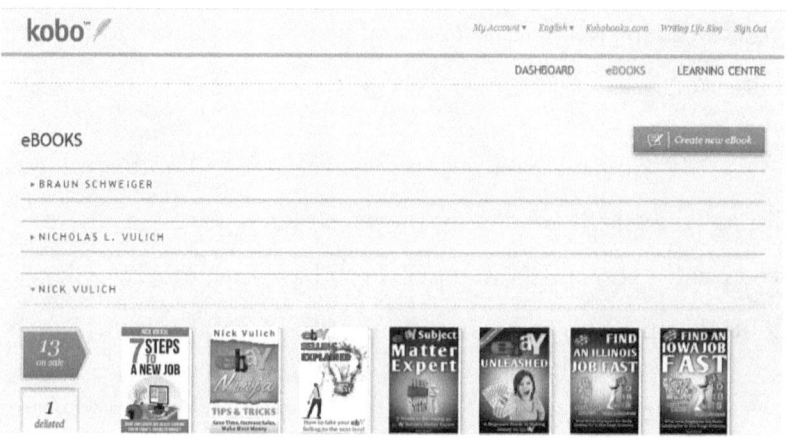

Select the green tab that says *create new book*. Listing your book is broken down into five steps.

1. Describe your eBook
2. Add eBook content
3. Choose content rights
4. Set the price
5. Publish your eBook

The form is intuitive and easy to use.

Fill in your title, subtitle, and series name if your book is part of a series. Under author, list your name, or the pen name you write under. The great thing is Kobo sets up a separate section with the books published under each author name, so you can keep your books separated by each pen name you write under.

If you have your own publisher name or imprint you can list it. Towards the middle of the page there's a section where you can list your ISBN number if you have one, otherwise leave it blank and Kobo will assign an identifier for your book.

Across from the ISBN information, there's a spot where you can add categories for your book. Kobo lets you select three categories. Try to use all three of them.

At the very bottom of the page you enter your synopsis or book description. Kobo doesn't allow you to use HTML, but they do have a formatting tool similar to MS Word where you can bold or italicize content. There's also a tool to add bullet points or line numbers to your description.

Moving back up towards the top of the page, click on the cover box to upload your cover image.

Click next to move to the section labeled *Add eBook content*. This is where you upload your book file. Kobo accepts your manuscript in the following formats – .epub, .doc, .docx, mobi, and .odt. After you upload your book file you can check it out by selecting *download and preview this eBook*. If everything looks good, click on next to move to the next section.

Choose content rights lets you select your book rights. Digital Rights Management (DRM) protects your book from copying and pirating. Geographic rights helps Kobo determine where you have legal rights to sell your book.

Click on *Save and next* to move to the next section. This is where you set your prices. To receive the 70 percent royalty you need to price your book between $1.99 and $12.99 in U S Dollars. If you price your book under $1.99, or over $12.99 you will receive a 45 percent royalty. As you set your prices, Kobo shows the royalty percentage and dollar amount in the two far right columns. You can set all of your geographic prices based on the U S price, or you can set a separate price for each geographic area.

This section also lets you set special promotional prices. Click on Select promo price, and it brings up a new section to set up your promo prices. First off, you need to select the special promo price, and then choose the start and end dates for your promo. You can set up your special in all territories, or choose just one geographic area for your promo.

After you've finished setting up your pricing, click *Save and next*. This takes you to the final section where you publish your book. You can select the date you want your book to go live, or just click the green *Publish* button and your book will go on sale as soon as Kobo finishes reviewing your book (normally 12 to 24 hours).

. . . .

If you need to edit your book or change prices, go to the section labeled eBooks, and select the book you want to change. Make your changes, and when you're finished click publish. Most changes filter through the system in under an hour, but it can take twelve hours or more.

. . . .

I'm still fairly new to Kobo so I can't give you any advice on what sales are like. I've heard people say their sales were good, especially in Canada.

DASHBOARD

| | June 2014 | This month |

SALES AT A GLANCE   SALES BY BOOK   SALES BY REGION

STATS FOR JUNE 2014   ALL TIME

0 eBooks sold   *1* eBooks sold

$0.⁰⁰ estimated earnings $2.⁷⁹ estimated earnings

1 titles published   *0* countries purchased in   *8* free downloads

To receive a 70 percent royalty you need to price your book between $1.99 and $12.99 in U S Dollars. If you price below $1.99, or over $12.99 you receive a 45 percent royalty. That's ten percent higher than you get from Amazon for pricing books outside of their sweet spot. If you have a paperback version of your book, Kobo requires you to price the Kobo version at least 20 percent lower than the physical copy to receive their maximum royalty payment.

One other thing to keep in mind is Kobo deducts taxes from your royalties when books are sold in European countries. They take 20 percent for the VAT tax in Great Britain, and 3 percent for the VAT tax in countries within the European Union. As a result, it is suggested you mark your prices up by this amount when selling in these countries. The *Kobo Writing Life User* Guide has more complete information on this.

Royalty payments are paid out monthly if your royalties are over $100 for the month. If you don't reach the $100 level in a six month period, they will pay out what you have earned up to that point. Funds are deposited directly into the bank account you placed on file when signing up.

Lulu

Lulu is similar to Amazon. It's a self-publishing platform and a marketplace for eBooks and physical books. Authors have the choice of uploading eBooks, paperbacks, or hardback books, and making them available exclusively on Lulu or on other platforms

The reason I decided to publish on Lulu is they offer an easy and relatively inexpensive method for making your books available in hardback.

My original plan was to do a Kickstarter campaign to launch a new book, and use a special hardbound series as a premium giveaway for larger donations. In the meantime I made six of my books available in hardback. When you select the globalREACH retail distribution plan with Lulu it makes your books available through Ingram, Amazon, Barnes and Noble, and other online book stores.

The real problem when you go to publish a hardbound book is price.

My bestselling book is *eBay 2014*. It has 122 pages. If I price it at $49.95, my royalties are $10.11. If I price it at $39.99 my royalties are $6.11. If I set it at Lulu's absolute minimum price of $24.68 I don't make any royalties when it is sold through globalREACH distribution. If I sell the book for $49.95 on Lulu I make $27.97—not too shabby. I can also offer different discounts to buyers who purchase the book on Lulu. For example if I offer a 20 percent discount, the book would sell for $39.95, and my royalty would be $17.97. That's still not too bad, if I were to make any sales on Lulu. But, that hasn't happened.

The same book in paperback on Amazon sells regularly for $15.99, and brings me a royalty of $7.33.

So why publish your book in hardback, if you're not doing it for money? Personal satisfaction was a driving force for me to release my books in a hardbound edition. I'm old school. Readers from my generation didn't consider a book to be a real book unless it was published in a hardbound edition. When I was a kid and my favorite books came out I'd grab them in the book club edition, or wait that long six months or a year for the paperback release. (Yeah! I really am that old.)

You may have an entirely different reason for wanting to produce a hardbound copy of your book. Whatever your reason, Lulu offers print-on-demand hardcover books at prices any author can afford. If you want, you can buy a single copy. I purchased proof copies of my books for $13.00 to $15.00 each, plus shipping. At this price most authors can afford to buy a copy for mom, dad, close friends, and maybe even a few extra copies to impress reviewers. I even considered ordering five or ten extra copies to send into Amazon to sell through their FBA program. I could price them at $35.00 each, and still make a little over $10.00 a copy.

. . . .

Publishing Your Book on Lulu

Lulu has an option on the front page of their website labeled *publish books for free*. Select it to get started making your book.

After this you are shown several formats available for you to produce your book in as well as sample costs and royalties for each type of book. Once you decide on the type of book you want to create, choose *Make Book* or *Make eBook* at the bottom of the page.

The next step is to select the type of book you want to make. Click on the one that corresponds to the book you want to make.

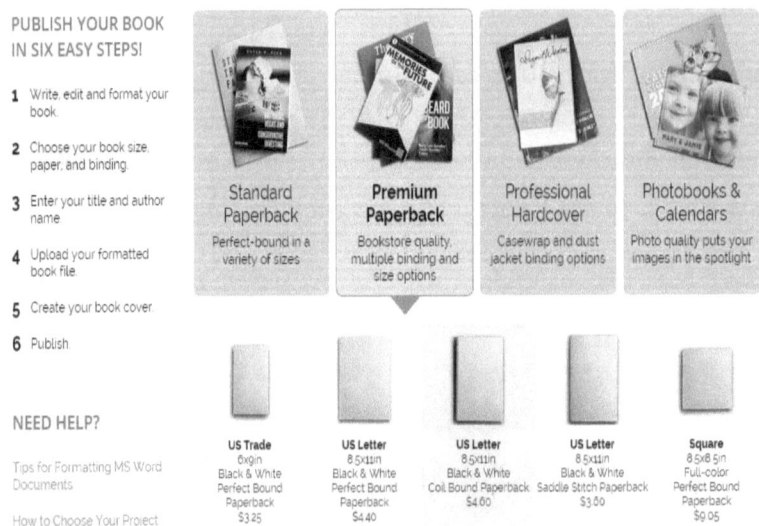

The next screen collects basic information about your book—title, author, and distribution methods. (You can make your book available to the world, or make it available just to you. The choice is yours.) After this you choose an ISBN. My suggestion is to choose a free ISBN from Lulu, otherwise you can add an ISBN you already own, or choose to proceed without an ISBN. If you assign an ISBN number to your book, be sure to write it down. If you want to make your book available through Lulu's globalREACH program you are required to add the book's ISBN number to the copyright page in a certain format. If you do this incorrectly you will have to reformat the book, and order another sample.

After this you upload your book files.

If you had your book formatted for a 6 x 9 Create Space paperback you can upload the same file to Lulu. It will have the proper formatting for their standard hardbound and paperback books. If your book hasn't been properly formatted, you will need to format it to the proper size. The easiest way to do this is to create a MS Word file, or hire a formatter on Fiverr to do it for you. Lulu has professional formatting options available to, but they will cost you much more than having it done on Fiverr.

Lulu accepts your book in a number of different formats including PDF, Doc, Docx, and others. After you upload it, you need to select *Make Print Ready File* on the next page. This creates the file Lulu will use to make your book. You are given the option to preview it so you can check for formatting errors.

When you are happy with your book file select *Save and Continue.* This will take you to the section where you create the dust jacket for your book.

If you're just looking for a basic dust jacket, you can design it yourself using Lulu's book cover creator. Pictures are uploaded in the tray on the right side of the page. After that you can drag and drop them into the appropriate spaces on your dust jacket. To add text, click on the white text tabs and type in your blurbs.

If you're looking for a more professional design I would suggest hiring an experienced designer on Fiverr or Elance.

The next page lets you preview your cover. When you're happy with it select *Make Print-Ready Cover* at the bottom of the page.

When you're finished creating your book cover Lulu asks you to describe your project. First you need to select a category. You're only allowed to pick one, so choose the most appropriate category for your book. Next you need to add the keywords readers will search for on Lulu to find your book. Be sure to separate each keyword phrase with a comma. Your description needs to be between 50 and 1,000 characters, so if you are copying your description from Amazon you may have to cut it down a bit. The rest of the fields are pretty self-explanatory—language, copyright info, license, edition, and publisher. The only field that could be tricky is license. If you're in doubt choose, *Standard Copyright License.*

Now you set your project price. You can play around with it a little until you find a price you think is right. The form shows you how much you will make at each retail price if your book sells on Lulu, or with globalREACH distribution. You can also set a discount for sales on Lulu. This lowers your royalties, but can make your books more attractive to buyers.

The final step is to review the information you entered for your book. Everything is presented on a review page. If you need to change something, select edit and make your changes. If everything looks good, give the go ahead to publish your book.

At this point your book is for sale to buyers on Lulu.

If you want to make your book available through globalREACH distribution where it is available through Ingram, Amazon, Barnes and Noble, and other distributors you have to jump a few more hurdles. First you need to purchase a sample copy of the book. After you receive your sample you need to return to your My Projects page to approve it. If you make any changes to your book after reviewing the sample copy you need to order another proof and then approve it.

. . . .

Sales wise, there's not much I can tell you about Lulu. I've only made two sales in the last four months. But remember, most of the books I created are hardbound editions that retail for $49.95 each. The story might be different if I had created lower priced paperback books or eBooks.

Experiment for yourself to decide if a hardbound edition is on tap for one of your books.

Final Wrap-up

To be a successful author today, you need to be a jack-of-all-trades.

You need to be an author, an editor, a businessman, and a self-publisher. You need to know how readers digest your book. You need to understand how to leverage different publishing platforms to your advantage. You need to develop a business and marketing plan for your books, and you need to work your plan for all it's worth.

One thing you should understand after reading this book is I don't advise going it entirely alone. By all means you should outsource some of the tasks you dislike, don't understand, or don't have time to learn. Sure, you can probably figure out how to format a book for Smashwords, but why put yourself through the hassle when someone else will do it for five bucks? The same thing goes for formatting your book for Create Space. I can do an OK job, but for fifteen bucks someone else will do an exceptional job. Why shouldn't I let them do it?

To be successful, you need to concentrate on what you're good at – Writing your books. To sell more books, you need to learn everything you can about self-publishing. And, to be really successful, you need to assemble a team that can keep pushing your books forward.

. . . .

Finally, I want to say I understand the struggle you're going through. It's not an easy decision to pull your books out of KDP. There is extra income from borrows, and Kindle Countdown Deals can bring in several hundred dollars each time you run them. *Kindle Unlimited* is a huge money-maker for most authors.

Leaving Amazon is a gamble.

There's no doubt about that. You'll still earn the regular income from your book sales, but there's nothing to fall back on when sales grow sluggish. And, they will. You can't supercharge them with free days or Countdown Deals. You can, however, run your own specials, marking them down to 99 cents for a few days, or longer.

Running frequent specials is one way authors can bolster sluggish sales. If you have an established author platform, you can promote specials on your website or blog. I've seen several kindle publishers drop their prices to 99 cents, and skyrocket their books to number one in their categories by blogging about the special. Jordan Malik did it three times during one six month period in the eBay category. He took three of his books and pulled them to number one, two, and three in the category.

If you have questions about using the 99 cent price point to drive sales, I'd suggest reading Steve Scott's book *Is 99 Cents the New Free?* Steve makes a convincing case for using this strategy. *Kindle unlimited* has slowed sales at that price point for many authors, but if you have an established author platform 99 cents is still an effective strategy for building sales.

Give it a shot, and see what a little self-promotion does for your book sales.

. . . .

Whatever happens, remember that ultimately you are responsible for the sales of your book.

I made two smart moves early on in my career that allowed me to succeed as a full time writer. The first was making my books available in paperback versions through Create Space. The paperback versions of my books normally earn between $1000 and $1500 per month in royalties.

The second move I made was making my books available as audio books through Audible (ACX). My books have only been available as audio books for six full months now, but I average $350 to $400 per month in royalties. By the end of the year I will have all of my books available as audio books, and expect to be earning between $500 and $600 per month in royalties with them.

. . . .

If you just finished reading this book and you're wondering which publishing platform you should try first, Create Space is a no brainer. People are always going to want paperback books. Audible is another great choice to start expanding your presence away from Kindle. If you choose the royalty share arrangement, your only out of pocket expense is for a cover, and can be as low as five bucks if you use a designer on Fiverr.

The other great thing about branching out with the help of Create Space and Audible (ACX) is they don't affect your exclusivity with Amazon, so you can still keep your books enrolled in KDP. It's when you start moving your books to other digital platforms that you will be forced to cut the cord with Amazon's KDP Program.

Read these Books Next

Congratulations for making your way through the entire book. Hopefully it has whetted your appetite to learn more about writing and self-publishing.

If you haven't made your books available on another platform, take some time out now to do that.

My recommendation is to build a library of books you can refer back to when you have questions or concerns about how to do something. If you're still unsure of what to do, reach out to other writers. They've been where you are, and many authors are willing to help others along on their journey—just ask.

Most importantly—read. Read about writing, read about self-publishing, marketing, and social media promotion. Read anything and everything you can get your hands on, because the more you read, the better you will become at writing.

Here are some of my choices of must have books.

. . . .

Self-Publisher's Legal Handbook. Helen Sedwick.

This book tackles many of the questions that plague self-publishers. Who owns the rights to your book cover—you, or your cover designer? What about copyright? How do you copyright your book, and is it necessary to file with the copyright office? What's involved in hiring a freelancer to design or co-author your book? And, what about taxes—what taxes do I owe, and how do I pay them.

Helen Sedwick does a great job of answering these questions. If you're a new or experienced self-publisher, this book is going to help you with business side of writing.

Public Speaking: Storytelling for Electrifying Presentations. Akash Karia.

This book is about how to deliver a great T.E.D. Talk, but all of the information in it is pertinent to writing. Karia is passionate about speaking, and has spent the last six years researching and listening to great presentations. The information he gives will help you structure and write more engaging books.

I don't want to give too many spoilers, but here's a short quote from early in the book. "Introduce the conflict early on…it gets your audience thinking, 'I wonder how this is going to end.'"

Yeah, the book is about public speaking, but this book is loaded with great advice that will help every writer pump up their books, and make them more engaging.

Shoot Your Novel: Cinematic Techniques to Supercharge Your Writing. C. S. Lakin.

The idea behind the book makes sense. If writers want to be successful, they should study Hollywood blockbusters. Good movies don't just happen. They're planned. They're edited to show exactly what the director wants viewers to see.

I don't want to give away the farm, so I'm only going to discuss a few camera shots.

One of these is the establishing shot. It occurs at the beginning of the movie, and when you are switching scenes. It establishes the locale, or gives viewers (readers) a frame of reference for the new scene. The establishing scene can be very brief, or it can take several minutes. It is important because it gives readers a context for what is going to happen. If you leave the establishing scene out, you risk confusing your readers.

Another important scene is the close-up. In the author's words, "…small close-up details can help make the scene come alive. Sensory details (touch, taste, sounds, sights, smells) are the most effective ways to make a scene come alive in the reader's mind."

How I Sold 30,000 eBooks on Amazon's Kindle. Martin Crosbie.

Best piece of advice, "Everything leads to something else, and you never know who might be reading your work or watching your career." For Martin, writing books led to speaking, teaching, and writing more books. Who knows where your writing will take you. His other advice is similar to that from all successful self-publishers – you're going to need more than one book, so keep writing.

I revisited this one again last night, and I really think every author needs to spend some time with it. Martin's attitude is really remarkable. I've said it before, and I'm going to repeat it again. Everything he talks about involves giving freely to help newer authors learn the trade. Each step along the way he tried new things and reached out to help others. Each time he did this new doors opened up for him – writing, teaching, or some other method to help promote his books.

Like it. Hate it. It doesn't really matter. Just read it, and start giving back to move your career forward.

The Author Training Manual. Nina Amir.

Nina Amir has written three books that can really help Kindle self-publishers—*Authorpreneur*, *The Author Training Manual*, and *How to Blog A Book*. If you choose to read only one, read Authorpreneur. It is an abbreviated version of the other two books, and has the short version of most of the information contained in the other two books.

The *Author Training Manual* teaches writers to think about their writing as a business, and to approach self-publishing the way publishers approach selecting books. That means creating a business plan for your book. Trust me. The process isn't for the weak at heart. It takes a lot of hard work. You need to boil the essence of your book down to one or two sentences so you understand what it's about. You need to analyze the competition, and position your book so readers, publishers, and you know how it's different from other books out there. And, here's another toughie. You need to establish why you're the best person to write your book. The good thing is: if you do these things, you're in a better position to write and publish a successful book.

How to Blog a Book examines how to do just that, create a blog, and have your book grow out of it. For writers this helps do several things. 1) If you don't already have an author platform, it allows you to build one as you write your book. 2) It makes you commit to writing regularly. And, 3) it gives you a way to get immediate feedback on your book. This way you can make changes as you go, or scrap the project if you discover it's not working.

Let's Get Digital. David Gaughran.

For many authors and publishers David Gaughran is the go to guy for self-publishing information. This book was revised and rewritten in October of 2014, and is one of the most up-to-date sources on self-publishing.

Gaughran hits on all of the topics important to self-publishers—price, platform, Amazon, Print-on-Demand using Create Space, and publishing scams. Perhaps the most enlightening section of the book covers Amazon's algorithms. What's involved in creating a best-seller? How do you get your book moving and jumping up the charts in Amazon's ecosystem? If you're in the dark about how Amazon promotes your book, this section will answer all of your questions.

Gaughran's other book *Let's Get Visible* discusses how to get your book noticed on Amazon. If you've ever felt like your book is lost amongst the millions of other titles available on Amazon, this book will unravel some of the mysteries for you. It will help you get the basics in order to give your books the best chance of being successful.

Supercharge Your Kindle Sales. Nick Stephenson.

This book does two things very well. 1) It explains Amazon's algorithms, and 2) It gives one of the best explanations I've come across on how to choose and employ keywords to make your books more successful.

Here's the least you need to know. Amazon looks at keywords to decide which books they should show readers. The keywords they use to recommend your book don't just come from the seven keywords you enter in KDP. Amazon also looks for keywords in your title, subtitle, series title, book description, and in customer reviews.

If you want your book to be found, you need to ensure you include the correct keywords in each of these places. Here's a quote from the author, "A book with highly targeted keywords will last a lot longer, because Amazon will promote it to readers who are looking for books just like yours."

Is 99 Cents the New Free? Steve Scott.

Steve Scott has written extensively about Kindle publishing. If anyone out there could be labeled the "guru" of self-publishing, it would probably be Steve. His books are short, easy to read, and cover one topic in detail, which is exactly the advice he gives readers about how to write Kindle books.

In *Is 99 Cents the New Free* Scott looks at price points and how they affect sales. One thing most writers understand is free is not as effective as it used to be. Another problem with free books is that there is a large group of people who download them just because they are free, with no intention of ever reading them. Scott also examines a second group of Kindle readers who load up on free books and subsequently leave negative reviews for books they downloaded for free. One reason he speculates for this is when readers download free books they often select books they normally wouldn't read. As a result you get one and two star reviews that say, "It didn't apply to me." Or, "Not what I was looking for."

That's the bad stuff that can happen. The good stuff is 99 cents is a great price point to launch new books, and recharge books that have lost steam. Read the book and see if Steve's advice can help you out.

How to Write Irresistible Stories. David Ho.

This is a short book aimed more at fiction writers, but it's got some good stuff in it and is worth reading.

The most important point I came across was to "Know your genre. Get familiar with the writing styles, story structures, how the characters are introduced, what types of conflicts are used…"

It just makes sense readers buy genre books expecting them to follow a pattern. If you break the rules for your type of story, you're going to disappoint your readers, and discourage repeat sales.

Another piece of advice you can use for fiction or non-fiction. "There are only so many different kinds of stories out there…You have to learn to do a different take on them…Add a new twist. Find a new way to tell the story."

How to Market a Book. Joanna Penn.

If you're at a loss about how to market your book, this book would be a good first stop. What I like best is Penn doesn't tell you you have to do this, this, and this. Instead she says these are things that have been helpful for myself and other authors. If you feel uncomfortable using this marketing method don't use it.

The best piece of advice in the book comes early on: "…most people aren't interested or won't like your book. The trick is to find the group of people who will be interested."

Easier said than done, right?

The first section covers the basics of your book, because if you don't have them right no amount of marketing is going to sell your work. That means you need to target your book to the right audience. You need to have a genre specific book cover that relates to your book's topic. You need a relevant book description that makes people want to read your book, and just as important—your look inside sample needs to hook readers and make them want to know more.

If you've got the basics right, then you can explore the rest of the book and learn the different methods available to you to market your book effectively.

Let's just say, if your book isn't selling, or you're struggling to move one or two copies a week, Joanna Penn has the advice you need to sell more books.

Before you go

Thank you for reading this book. If you enjoyed it, or found it helpful, I'd be grateful if you'd post a short review. Your review really does help. It helps other readers decide if this book would be a good investment for them, and it helps me to make this an even better book for you. I personally read all of the reviews my books receive, and based on what readers tell me, I can make my books even better, and include the kind of information readers want and need.

Please take a moment to return to the site where you purchased this book to leave a short review..

Thanks again for choosing my book, and here's wishing you great success in your writing.

Books by Nick Vulich

eBay 2014: Why You're Not Selling Anything on eBay, and What you Can Do About it

Freaking Idiots Guide to Selling on eBay: How Anyone Can Make $100 or More Everyday Selling on eBay

Sell it Online: How to Make Money Selling on eBay, Amazon, Fiverr, & Etsy

Audio Books by Nick Vulich

eBay 2014: Why Your Stuff Isn't Selling And What You Can Do About It

Freaking Idiots guide to Selling on eBay: How anyone can make $100 or more everyday selling on eBay